Original title:
Through the Tears

Copyright © 2024 Swan Charm
All rights reserved.

Author: Olivia Oja
ISBN HARDBACK: 978-9916-89-685-3
ISBN PAPERBACK: 978-9916-89-686-0
ISBN EBOOK: 978-9916-89-687-7

Heartstrings of Faith

In shadows deep, we seek the light,
With every prayer, our souls take flight.
Through trials faced, our hearts entwine,
In sacred trust, Your love will shine.

When storms arise, we hold our ground,
In whispered hopes, Your grace is found.
With faith as shield, we stand as one,
Embracing life, until we're done.

Reviving the Hopeful Spirit

Awake, arise, O spirit bold,
In weary hearts, ignite the gold.
With each new dawn, a chance bestowed,
To walk the path, where love has flowed.

Beneath the weight of sorrow's chain,
A flicker shines, through grounded pain.
In trust's warm embrace, we mend the seams,
Together we'll weave, our wildest dreams.

The Tapestry of Grief

In woven threads, our sorrows blend,
Each tear a note, each laugh a mend.
Through shadowed paths, we find the grace,
In every heart, You leave a trace.

Though time may dim the brightest star,
In memory's glow, we heal the scar.
With love that binds, we move ahead,
In unity, our spirits spread.

Sacred Melodies from Murmurs

In quiet whispers, a song begins,
A melody born from where love spins.
With every note, the world can hear,
The sacred story, the hearts we cheer.

As echoes linger, through valleys low,
We find the strength, in ebb and flow.
For in each sigh, the spirit breathes,
With love's sweet hymn, our worry leaves.

Whispers in the Wilderness

In the stillness, the Spirit sighs,
Guiding souls through shadowed skies.
Broken dreams upon the ground,
In whispered love, true peace is found.

The trees stand tall, their arms raised high,
Cradling prayers that drift and fly.
In the silence, hearts ignite,
With gentle whispers, we seek the light.

Mountains echo with ancient grace,
Each stone a promise, a sacred place.
Streams of faith flow, crystal clear,
In wilderness, the Spirit draws near.

Sunset bleeds into twilight's frame,
A symphony of hope, calling His name.
Through the night, let courage bloom,
In His presence, dispelling gloom.

And when dawn breaks, a new hymn sings,
Embracing life as the morning brings.
In every shadow, light will break,
In whispers soft, new paths we'll take.

Echoing the Eternal Hope

In the heart of night, a lantern glows,
Casting warmth where the spirit flows.
Every tear, a seed that's sown,
From silence, beauty has grown.

Majestic mountains reach for the skies,
Where faith remains, and courage flies.
In every voice, a song of grace,
Resounding love in this sacred place.

The stars declare a promise bright,
Guiding souls through the dark of night.
With each heartbeat, hope would rise,
A glimpse of Heaven in our eyes.

Paths may twist and wander far,
Yet in the distance, shines our star.
In every sorrow, joy will dance,
In every struggle, a second chance.

Oh, eternal hope, in shadows dwell,
A guiding beacon, a gentle bell.
Through trials fierce, our spirits soar,
In love divine, forevermore.

Canticles of the Enduring Spirit

In the stillness of the night,
Hope whispers soft and light.
Voices rise to heavenly tune,
Guiding souls beneath the moon.

Through trials deep and shadowed paths,
The spirit sings amidst the wrath.
Each tear a drop of sacred grace,
Embracing all, in love's embrace.

With each dawn, a promise new,
A testament to break on through.
Faith avows, despite despair,
In every heart, a vibrant prayer.

In the garden where hearts mend,
Love's enduring light extends.
Miracles in every breath,
Transcending life, transforming death.

Shadows of the Holy Cry

In the shadows, echoes call,
A voice of truth that pierces all.
Through the silence, spirits soar,
Yearning for an open door.

In every wound, a sign of grace,
In the dark, we find our place.
Hearts entwined in sacred trust,
Rising up from sacred dust.

Each sorrow shared, a path to light,
In unity, hearts take flight.
Every whisper, every sigh,
A gathering of faith, we cry.

In the shadows, love remains,
Binding hearts with gentle chains.
Faithful hands, together raised,
In holy light, we are praised.

Prayers Woven from Broken Halos

In the fragments of our souls,
We gather dreams, we mend, we hold.
Each broken piece, a golden thread,
In chaos, prayers are fed.

From the ashes, spirits rise,
Transforming pain into the skies.
A tapestry of love reborn,
In sorrow's depth, new hope is worn.

Glimmers shine from shattered light,
Reflections of a holy fight.
In every prayer, a story spins,
From broken halos, healing begins.

Hands united, lifting high,
In silent reverence, we comply.
With every heartbeat, love will flow,
In the garden, hope will grow.

Spiritual Rebirth in the Fragments

Amidst the shards, the spirit gleams,
In every fracture, hope redeems.
With whispers soft, the heart will mend,
In the fragments, life transcends.

The dawn breaks through the shadows deep,
Awakening dreams, and souls will leap.
In every splinter, divine grace,
Crafting joy in every place.

With each step, the new path clears,
Wiping away the doubts and fears.
Rising up on wings of light,
In the darkness, spirits unite.

Through storms of doubt, we find our way,
Faith illuminating each new day.
In the fragments, beauty lies,
Ever steadfast beneath the skies.

The Stone and the Light

Upon the stone, through shadows cast,
The light emerges, a guide steadfast.
It whispers hope, in darkest night,
A beacon shining, banishing fright.

Each soul it touches, a spark ignites,
Transforming burdens to heavenly heights.
In faith we stumble, in grace we rise,
The stone, a pathway to endless skies.

Hold tightly, child, to the warmth of love,
For in its embrace, the light above.
Obscured by trials, yet still so bright,
A sacred promise, the endless light.

A Journey of Lost Innocence

In gardens once fragrant, now sorrowed cries,
The echoes of laughter, lost in the sighs.
With footsteps uncertain, we tread the path,
Searching for solace in aftermath.

The sun fades slowly, the colors bleed,
In shadows we ponder, the heart's deep need.
With each passing moment, the child within,
Yearns for the purity shrouded in sin.

Yet hope is a river, flowing so free,
It carries the weary, to shores of esprit.
With courage ignited, we rise from the fall,
A journey of wisdom, a gift to us all.

Pilots of Pain

Through storms we navigate, with heavy hearts,
Pilots of pain, where sorrow starts.
The skies may darken, the thunder roll,
Yet steady we sail, with our fractured soul.

In the realm of anguish, strength is found,
A tender resilience, in grief profound.
With scars as our maps, we chart the way,
Guided by shadows, till break of day.

In unity's harbor, we find our rest,
Each wound a story, each trial a test.
Together we stand, through heartache and strife,
As pilots of pain, we reclaim our life.

Celestial Tears

Stars shed their brilliance, like tears in the night,
Celestial whispers, all shimmering white.
Each droplet descends, with stories to share,
Of love everlasting, transcending despair.

In the silence, we gather, beneath the vast sky,
With eyes raised in wonder, we question the why.
Yet wisdom drifts softly, like clouds in the breeze,
Reminding our spirits, our hearts find their ease.

For every teardrop that falls from above,
Is a thread in the tapestry, woven with love.
In the fabric of fate, our souls intertwine,
Celestial tears, a blessing divine.

Earthly Reflections

In the mirror of earth, our shadows are cast,
Reflecting the moments, both present and past.
With every sunrise, the truth is revealed,
In earthly reflections, our hearts are healed.

The winds speak of journeys, both sorrow and grace,
In the whispers of nature, we find our place.
Mountains stand witness, to time's gentle flow,
As rivers of memories continue to grow.

In stillness, we ponder, the cycles of life,
A dance intertwined, with joy and with strife.
Let wisdom be born from each twist and turn,
In earthly reflections, our spirits will learn.

Sacrificial Love and Despair

In the shadow of the cross,
He bore our pain and loss.
With crimson tears, love bled,
For every soul, His heart was shed.

Whispers of hope in darkened nights,
Through anguish come the purest lights.
Each thorn and wound, a story told,
In love's embrace, both meek and bold.

Despair may rise like a stormy sea,
Yet in His grace, we find the key.
To rise anew from ashes deep,
In sacrificial love, our hearts we keep.

Love that gives till the end is near,
Brings forth strength to conquer fear.
Through trials, He calls us to stand,
In His embrace, we meet His hand.

So let our hearts with courage fight,
To mirror His unfailing light.
For in our wounds, His love shall grow,
In sacrificial love, we find our glow.

The Weaving of Wounds

In the tapestry of our scars,
Love weaves bright amidst the jars.
Threads of sorrow, strands of grace,
In every wound, a holy space.

He stitches pain with threads of gold,
Each tear a tale of love retold.
With gentle hands, He mends our night,
In darkness, we rediscover light.

The loom of life, both fierce and kind,
Through every ache, His hand we find.
He gathers fragments, broken, torn,
From every wound, new hearts are born.

As colors blend in sacred art,
We find the healing of the heart.
For every wound, a prayer takes flight,
In love's embrace, we find our might.

Together woven, we shall stand,
In faith and hope, united hand in hand.
For in the fabric of His love, we grow,
In the weaving of wounds, His mercy flows.

Silent Prayers Underneath the Weight

Beneath the weight of sorrow's veil,
We lift our hearts in quiet trail.
Silent prayers like whispers rise,
In the stillness, hope implies.

The burdens heavy on the soul,
Yet in His arms, we find our whole.
Each sigh, a gift, each tear, a plea,
In His embrace, we long to be.

He hears the cries when silence reigns,
In every struggle, love remains.
With patient grace, He bears our shame,
Transforming loss, igniting flame.

In quiet moments, strength appears,
Our faith grows deep through hidden fears.
Each prayer, a beacon in the night,
Guiding us towards the light.

So let us trust when shadows fall,
For in our weakness, He hears our call.
In silent prayers, our spirits soar,
Underneath the weight, we're not ignored.

The Cup of Sacrificial Sorrow

In the garden, shadows loom,
He chose to face the bitter bloom.
The cup of sorrow, deep and wide,
With love's embrace, our fears collide.

Each drop, a taste of sacrifice,
For every soul, He paid the price.
With heavy heart and burdened brow,
He drank the pain, we know not how.

In communion, pain reveals
The depths of love that softly heals.
With open hearts, we gather near,
To share the cup, to shed our fear.

His sorrow holds a sacred grace,
In every tear, a holy place.
For though He bore our darkest night,
In sacrificial love, we find our light.

So let us lift the cup in prayer,
Remembering the love we share.
For in our grief, we're never alone,
In the cup of sorrow, our hearts find home.

The Weight of Compassion

In silence, love's tender grace,
We gather our hearts, a holy place.
With every burden we bear and share,
Compassion blooms, a sacred flare.

Through trials deep, our spirits rise,
In whispered prayers, we seek the skies.
Each tear a river, flowing wide,
In love's embrace, we'll abide.

With gentle hands, we lift the meek,
In humble strength, a voice we speak.
For in the darkest hours we find,
The light of hope, forever kind.

Beneath the weight of sorrow's chain,
We offer solace in the pain.
A steadfast heart, a guiding star,
Compassion guides us, near and far.

Together we weave a tapestry
Of mercy's arms surrounding thee.
In every challenge, we will stand,
For love transcends, a holy band.

Sculpted by Sorrow

From shadows cast, our spirits grow,
In sorrow's grip, we learn to sow.
Each trial faced, a sculptor's hand,
Shapes our hearts on shifting sand.

The tears we shed, like gentle rain,
Nurture seeds of love from pain.
In fractured places, beauty blooms,
A sacred light in darkened rooms.

Hearts entwined, we rise as one,
Finding strength in battles won.
In every scar, a story told,
Of courage forged, and faith bold.

Each moment lost, a lesson found,
In quiet whispers, grace abounds.
Through sorrow's dance, we learn to see,
The strength within, wild and free.

Embrace the journey, let it unfold,
For in our hearts, the truth is gold.
Sculpted by sorrow, we learn to shine,
In love's embrace, forever divine.

Resurrections from Ruin

In crumbled stones, life springs anew,
From ashes rise, the spirit too.
Hope's gentle whisper calls us near,
Rebirth awaits, through love and fear.

With every fall, a promise made,
In darkness deep, our path is laid.
From shattered dreams, we forge ahead,
In unity, our spirits wed.

Through trials faced, our hearts ignite,
In courage found, we claim our light.
Resurrection blooms in sacred ground,
A symphony of grace profound.

Together we mend, with hands outstretched,
In love's embrace, our souls refreshed.
Through every tear, a testament stands,
Of rising strong, united hands.

In ruin's wake, we chant our song,
For through it all, we still belong.
With every heartbeat, we proclaim,
Our lives reborn, forever flame.

The Crucible of Comfort

In the furnace of trials, we stand tall,
Forged by fire, together we call.
The crucible's heat refines our way,
In comfort's grace, we choose to stay.

In gentle whispers, love surrounds,
Each heart's lament, a sacred sound.
Through every struggle, we find our peace,
A balm for wounds that never cease.

With arms wide open, we share our light,
In darkest moments, our faith ignites.
Together we journey, through thick and thin,
Finding solace, where love begins.

The comfort found in shared despair,
Creates a bond, a sacred prayer.
In trials faced, we draw our strength,
In compassion's depth, we find our length.

From every ashes, we rise anew,
In love's embrace, our spirits grew.
The crucible of comfort, our shared design,
In unity and grace, our hearts align.

Glistening Stones of Sorrow's Journey

In valleys deep where shadows dwell,
Glistening stones sing of tales they tell.
Whispers rise on the breath of night,
Hearts burdened seek the light.

Each stone a tear of silent grace,
Marking the path in this solemn space.
Bearing the weight of weary dreams,
Guided by hope's gentle beams.

From sorrows past, we find our way,
Through trials faced, in night and day.
The journey long, yet spirit strong,
In the arms of faith, we belong.

In every ache, a lesson learned,
A spark of joy amidst the burned.
Together we rise, our voices blend,
In the sacred bond, we shall transcend.

Look to the stones, their glimmer bright,
For they hold truths bathed in light.
With every step, we draw near,
To the solace found in love's pure sphere.

The Unseen Angel's Grief

In silence we walk, the veil so thin,
Guided by faith from deep within.
An unseen angel weeps above,
Crying for those who've lost their love.

Through darkened skies, a sorrowed tune,
Fills the night, beneath the moon.
For every heart that feels the sting,
The angel's song begins to ring.

Softly the breeze carries each sigh,
A testament to those who cry.
We feel the weight of their despair,
Yet know the angel lingers there.

In every tear, a sacred prayer,
An echo of love that fills the air.
With every breath, we hold them tight,
In the shadowed corners of the night.

Together we lift our spirits high,
Under the arch of the endless sky.
For though they're gone, they never part,
In memories held within the heart.

Clarity in the Valley of Shadows

In the valley where shadows play,
We seek clarity to light the way.
With every step, we face our fears,
Finding strength through endless tears.

The whispers of doubt may cloud the mind,
Yet in the silence, hope we find.
For even in the darkest night,
Stars emerge, a guiding light.

Like rivers flowing through ancient stone,
Our spirits rise, no longer alone.
In the depths of sorrow, wisdom grows,
A tender heart, and peace bestows.

In unity, we lift our prayer,
For those caught in despair's snare.
With open hearts, we break the chain,
Finding solace in our pain.

We walk as one, through shadows cast,
A journey shared, the die is cast.
Clarity shines as we press on,
In the valley of shadows, hope is born.

Sacred Echoes Beyond the Veil

Across the veil, where spirits roam,
Sacred echoes call us home.
In every heartbeat, whispers rise,
Tales of love that never dies.

The world may fade, yet bonds remain,
In memories etched through joy and pain.
With every breath, their presence near,
A testament to love so clear.

In the quiet moments, we recall,
The laughter shared, the rise, the fall.
For in their light, we find our way,
Guided by love that will not sway.

In the dance of time, we intertwine,
Echoes of the sacred, pure and fine.
Together we sing, our voices blend,
In the rhythm of souls that never end.

Embrace the day, hold close the night,
For every heart will find its light.
Beyond the veil, we shall unite,
In sacred echoes, love ignites.

The Light of Tomorrow in Every Tear

In sorrow's depth, we find the grace,
Each tear a path to a holy space.
The light of dawn breaks through the night,
Illuminating hope within our sight.

Through pain we walk, a sacred road,
With every struggle, wisdom bestowed.
For in the tears that freely flow,
We glimpse the strength we come to know.

In quiet moments, we seek His face,
Finding solace in His warm embrace.
With every burden, a chance to rise,
Transforming grief into the skies.

The heart, though heavy, learns to sing,
With faith, the weary soul takes wing.
In every tear, a promise clear,
The light of tomorrow draws us near.

So now we stand, in love we trust,
For in His hands, we find our just.
Each tear a seed of grace in bloom,
A testament to love that breaks the gloom.

The Divine Flowering of Affliction

In darkened valleys, blossoms grow,
Affliction brings what we must know.
With every thorn, a chance to see,
The beauty sprouting from the tree.

Hearts intertwined in shared pain's song,
In suffering's grip, we learn to belong.
Each trial faced, a fragrant breath,
Awakening life amidst the death.

The rain of grief, a sacred gift,
Nurtures the souls that yearn to lift.
From ashes stirred, new hope will rise,
In the garden where the spirit flies.

We gather strength from roots so deep,
In the soil of sorrow, secrets keep.
From suffering grows the purest light,
Transforming darkness into bright.

Each petal born from night's embrace,
A reminder of love's gentle grace.
In the divine flowering we see,
Affliction blooms, setting our souls free.

Resilient Spirits in Unholy Spaces

In shadows cast by the world's design,
Resilient spirits boldly shine.
In unholy spaces, faith takes flight,
Guided by grace that ignites the night.

Through trials faced, our strength is found,
In cracked foundations, love abounds.
With every stumble, we rise anew,
With hearts ignited, fierce and true.

In chaotic storms, we hold the line,
With prayerful whispers, our voices intertwine.
Each struggle fought is a sacred dance,
An invitation to rise and advance.

Against the tide, we lift our gaze,
Finding in darkness the light that stays.
In unholy spaces, we reclaim our time,
And in the struggle, we find the climb.

So let us stand with spirits bold,
In every challenge, let faith unfold.
For even in shadows, we shall not fear,
Resilient hearts will always steer.

Whispers of the Silent Struggle

In the stillness, whispers arise,
Voices unheard beneath the skies.
The silent struggle bears its name,
Yet speaks of love in a tender flame.

For every heart that bears the weight,
In quiet resolve, we navigate fate.
With every sigh, a story shared,
A testament of how we have dared.

Amongst the noise, we find our peace,
In moments still, our fears release.
Each silent tear, a prayerful plea,
Uniting souls in vibrant spree.

Through shadows cast, our spirits soar,
In the silent struggle, we seek for more.
With whispered truths, we raise our song,
Finding strength where we all belong.

So listen closely to the softest sound,
For in the silence, our hope is found.
In the whispers of the silent fight,
We learn to trust in love's great light.

Sacred Tears of the Penitent

In shadows deep, I kneel and pray,
The weight of sin, I bear each day.
With sacred tears, I humbly plead,
For mercy's grace, my soul's true need.

The light above, it softly shines,
Illuminating sacred signs.
In brokenness, I find my way,
To rise anew, to trust the day.

As echoes of my failings fade,
In grace, I seek the plans, He laid.
To cleanse my heart, to wash my soul,
In love divine, I will be whole.

Each prayer a step toward the dawn,
In silence vast, the burdens gone.
With every tear, His love will flow,
Restoring joy that I once know.

The road is long, yet I embrace,
The hope of love, forgiveness' grace.
In sacred tears, my spirit sings,
In penitence, new life it brings.

Voices of the Afflicted

In the silence, cries arise,
Voices strong, yet filled with sighs.
The burdened heart, the weary soul,
In darkness deep, they seek the whole.

Each story told, a heavy chain,
Yet through the pain, they seek the gain.
In every tear, a yearning plea,
For hands to hold, for eyes to see.

The shadows whisper, tales of old,
In unity, the brave and bold.
Together now, we'll rise and cry,
For love that heals, for hope on high.

In valleys deep, we find our hymn,
With broken hearts, we sing for Him.
Each note a prayer, a bond of trust,
In faith we stand, in love we must.

Voices weave a tapestry,
Of pain transformed to victory.
In sacred space, our spirits rest,
With grace and strength, we are blessed.

The Gift of Vulnerability

To bare the heart is not easy,
Yet in this truth, we find what's free.
A tender soul, exposed to light,
In vulnerability, we ignite.

The walls we build, so high and strong,
Yet lead us to a path of wrong.
With open arms, let love embrace,
In every crack, a sacred place.

In gentle whispers, courage found,
As hearts connect, the world unbound.
For in our weakness, strength can rise,
A gift so rare, beneath the skies.

To share the load, to hold a hand,
In trust, together we shall stand.
In every tear, a story told,
An offering of love, more precious than gold.

The gift resides in honest eyes,
Where love can flourish, never dies.
In vulnerability, we'll learn to dance,
A sacred bond, a second chance.

Essence of Enduring Hope

When dawn emerges, soft and bright,
With whispers pure, it chases night.
In every heart, a flicker glows,
The essence of hope, forever flows.

Through trials faced, and storms we'll weather,
Bound by faith, we rise together.
With every step, the path we trace,
In hope, we find our sacred space.

Each dream we hold, a promise sweet,
A journey long, but we won't retreat.
With every tear that marks our face,
Hope's gentle hand will leave its grace.

As shadows fall, and doubts may creep,
In steadfast hearts, our secrets keep.
With every breath, we breathe anew,
In hope's embrace, life feels true.

In unity, we learn to soar,
With joyful hearts, we'll sing once more.
The essence of hope shall light the way,
In love divine, we find our day.

Pains Made Sacred in Quiet Reverie

In shadows deep, where sorrows lie,
A gentle grace begins to sigh.
Each tear a prayer, each wound a song,
In sacred silence, I belong.

The burdens borne, through nights of fear,
Transform to strength, as love draws near.
In quiet reverie, hope finds a way,
To turn the night into day.

With every ache, a lesson learned,
In hands of mercy, our spirits turned.
The pain may linger, but hearts will mend,
In whispered truths, we find our friend.

So let me dwell in this holy space,
Where hurt and healing share their grace.
For in the pause of grief and woe,
The essence of life begins to flow.

In sacred moments, as time unfolds,
A tapestry of faith is told.
In quietude, our spirits soar,
As pains made sacred, open doors.

A Tapestry Woven with Weeping

In the loom of life, threads intertwine,
Each drop of sorrow, a word divine.
A tapestry woven with pain and grace,
In every stitch, the shadowed face.

With hands outstretched to the skies above,
Each weeping moment, a sign of love.
The fabric thickens with stories untold,
In colors bright and edges bold.

Through threads of hope, the heart does sew,
In darkest valleys, new blossoms grow.
Each tear a color, rich and deep,
In the quilt of faith, our souls to keep.

Together we weave, through joy and strife,
A narrative sacred, rich as life.
In the pattern of pain, beauty will shine,
A tapestry forever divine.

As day breaks soft on woven dreams,
The weeping heart begins to beam.
In the fabric of love, we find our place,
And in every tear, behold His grace.

The Silent Sermon of the Soul

In the stillness, whispers arise,
A silent sermon that never dies.
With every heartbeat, the truth unfolds,
In sacred spaces, wisdom holds.

The aching silence, a canvas wide,
Where sorrow and solace gently reside.
In the depth of quiet, the soul does sing,
Of trials faced and the strength they bring.

Each breath a lesson, each moment a gift,
In silence profound, our spirits lift.
With every tear, clarity grows,
In the dark, the light always flows.

Through unspoken words, we hear His voice,
Guiding our hearts to make the choice.
In the sanctuary of trust, let us find,
The silent sermon that speaks to the mind.

For in the stillness, we gather peace,
A holy promise, a sweet release.
In every silence, may we be whole,
In the quiet depths of the yearning soul.

In the Quietude of Despair

In shadows thick, where sorrow dwells,
The heartache quiet, a story tells.
In the stillness deep, despair takes root,
Yet in this soil, new life can shoot.

With every whisper of the night,
A flicker of hope emerges bright.
In the quietude, the spirit sighs,
And through the tears, our courage flies.

In darkened hours, let faith ignite,
For even in gloom, the stars shine bright.
The weight of sorrow begins to lift,
In the quietude, we find our gift.

So in the depth, may we not fear,
For love resides, eternally near.
In the stillness, we hear His call,
And in our weakness, He holds us all.

Through quietude, our spirits rise,
From the depths, we learn to prize.
In the sacred hush of night and day,
Despair transforms, and hope will stay.

Reverent Pathways in the Darkness

In shadows deep, we start to tread,
With faith as light, we forge ahead.
Each step a prayer, each breath a plea,
For guidance from the One we see.

Through trials faced, our spirits soar,
In silence held, we seek evermore.
The heart whispers truths we long to find,
As grace unravels the ties that bind.

When doubts arise, we hold the flame,
In sacred trust, we call His name.
The road may bend, but we shall stand,
With open hearts and willing hands.

Awake, O soul, to mysteries great,
In reverence, we embrace our fate.
For every tear, a lesson bestowed,
In darkness, we find the light of hope.

With loving kindness along the way,
We walk as one with hearts in sway.
For in the night, we see His face,
In every shadow, we find grace.

A Blessing in the Brokenness

From shattered dreams, new hope can rise,
In brokenness, we touch the skies.
With tender hands, we weave the fray,
In love, our scars shall find their play.

In mournful nights, we hear the call,
Each crack reveals the light of all.
The heart learns well from trials passed,
And in our grief, God's peace is cast.

A blessing flows from every fall,
In loss, we hear the gentle thrall.
For when we're weak, His strength breaks through,
In every wound, the grace renews.

So let us gather, hand in hand,
To lift each other, understand.
In every tear, a truth untold,
In brokenness, our spirits' gold.

Through every storm, we'll find our way,
In faith we grow, come what may.
Together, rising from the night,
A blessing found in broken light.

Candlelight in the Midnight Hour

When darkness falls and silence creeps,
A flickering light in stillness weeps.
Candle flames dance, with whispers near,
In midnight's embrace, we lose our fear.

Each moment counts, a sacred time,
In solitude, we hear the chime.
The pulse of prayer, a steady beat,
In candlelight, we feel complete.

In flickers bright, hope finds its throne,
Where weary souls shall not walk alone.
Amid the night, a promise glows,
As wisdom through the darkness flows.

With thoughts uplifted, we seek divine,
In whispered breaths, our hearts entwine.
For every spark ignites the soul,
In midnight hours, we become whole.

So let the candle guide our way,
Through shadows cast, to brighter day.
In unity, our spirits rise,
With candlelight, we touch the skies.

Hymns of Healing in the Abyss

In depths profound, where few would tread,
We sing our hymns, though hearts feel led.
For in the void, a melody's born,
A healing song, where hope is worn.

With every note, the chains do break,
In sorrow's grip, our spirits wake.
Though shadows loom, we still proclaim,
In darkest hours, we lift His name.

The echoes of grace resound within,
Through trials faced, our souls begin.
In every struggle, we find our voice,
As healing hymns invite rejoice.

Through tears and pain, we learn to rise,
In faith's embrace, we find the ties.
The abyss may seem a daunting place,
Yet in the dark, we feel His grace.

So let our hearts be bold and free,
In hymns of healing, we find the key.
For even there, in depths we roam,
We sing of love, and make it home.

Psalm of Perseverance

In shadows deep, I tread the path,
Strength in spirit, whispers of faith.
Through trials fierce, I seek the light,
My heart finds peace in steadfast grace.

Though storms may come, I will not fear,
For in the night, Your love draws near.
Each step I take, You are my guide,
With every tear, my hope abides.

The road is long, yet I am strong,
For in Your arms, I do belong.
With outstretched hands, I seek the dawn,
And rise anew, my fears all gone.

When mountains loom, and valleys low,
Your gentle voice, a soft echo.
In whispered prayers, I place my trust,
For in Your name, my soul is just.

Through every trial, through every test,
I lift my eyes, my heart at rest.
In perseverance, I find my song,
For in Your love, I've known I belong.

In the Depths of Divine Despair

O Lord, I call in the dark of night,
My spirit aches, yet seeks Your light.
In shadows cast by sorrow deep,
I cling to hope when fears would creep.

Each whispered prayer, a fragile plea,
In quiet moments, I long for Thee.
When anguish strikes and faith feels frail,
I trust in promises that never pale.

Your grace, a balm for every wound,
In trials faced, my faith enshrouded.
Though storms may roar and tempests wail,
I find my strength within Your tale.

In depths of despair, I stand alone,
Yet know Your love has always shone.
With every heartbeat, I seek Your face,
In every tear, I find Your grace.

O guide my footsteps, steady and sure,
In darkness, Lord, Your love is pure.
For in this struggle, I'll rise and share,
The hope that's found in Divine care.

Cries of the Faithful Heart

With every beat, my heart does cry,
A song of love that soars on high.
Through trials faced, my spirit sings,
In trusting grace, my soul takes wings.

Your promises, like stars that shine,
Illuminate the path divine.
Though shadows fall and doubts assail,
In faithfulness, I shall prevail.

For in the pain, new strength is found,
In every fall, Your love abounds.
With prayers lifted, a guiding light,
I stand believing, through the night.

The faithful heart, though often pressed,
Finds solace in Your gentle rest.
With arms outstretched, I seek the shore,
A haven found forevermore.

In every cry, a hope reborn,
In weary days, my spirit worn,
Yet still I rise, with courage bright,
A testament to love's pure light.

Graceful Shadows of Suffering

In shadows deep, my spirit weeps,
Yet grace surrounds as silence keeps.
Through trials harsh, my heart must learn,
In every wound, a flame can burn.

The path is steep, the burdens great,
Yet in this pain, I find my fate.
Your gentle hand, a loving guide,
I walk with hope, in You abide.

Through suffering's storm, my faith takes flight,
Each tear I shed ignites the night.
For in the trials, wisdom grows,
In suffering's grip, true love bestows.

With every shadow, light does gleam,
In darkest hours, I cling to dream.
For grace abounds in each hard night,
And through my pain, I seek Your light.

In graceful shadows, I stand tall,
For in Your name, I'll never fall.
With faithful heart, I face the day,
In love and trust, I find my way.

The Veil Lifts in Silence

In quiet prayer, the heart ascends,
A whisper soft, where spirit bends.
The veil between worlds, gently sways,
Revealing grace in whispered ways.

In stillness found, the truth is born,
From night of doubt to light of morn.
With every sigh and breath we take,
The sacred bond, we dare not break.

A glow so warm, it fills the void,
In faith unshaken, we are buoyed.
The silence speaks, a holy song,
In every heart where we belong.

With lifted eyes, we seek the light,
In shadows past, now shining bright.
The veil that shrouds our weary soul,
In silence lifts, to make us whole.

Waters of Redemption Flow

In rivers deep, the waters cleanse,
A baptism pure, where sin suspends.
The current strong, it pushes through,
Redeeming love, forever true.

Each drop a promise, softly spoken,
In every wave, the chains are broken.
With faith we dip, our spirits rise,
In sacred depths, the heart replies.

The shores of grace, a gentle kiss,
In waters calm, we find our bliss.
The flow of mercy, ever near,
In every tear, a reflection clear.

From ancient wells, the blessings thrive,
In holy streams, we come alive.
The waters rush, forever free,
In love's embrace, our souls will be.

Grace Upon a Weeping Soul

In moments fraught with pain and strife,
A tender balm restores our life.
The tears we shed, like rivers stream,
In grace, we find our deepest dream.

Each heart that mourns, finds strength anew,
In gentle whispers, hope breaks through.
The weeping soul, in shadows cast,
Is cradled close, from first to last.

For every loss, a gift in disguise,
In sorrow's depths, the spirit flies.
With every ache, redemption sighs,
In love's embrace, the heart complies.

The dawn will break, the sun will rise,
Upon the tears, a sweet surprise.
In grace we stand, though tempest roll,
Forever blessed, a weeping soul.

In Shadows of Divine Mercy

In shadows deep, where sorrows dwell,
The light of mercy breaks the spell.
With open arms, the Savior stands,
Soothing hearts with gentle hands.

In trials faced, we seek His grace,
In every tear, we find our place.
The shadows whisper, yet we shine,
In divine mercy, love entwines.

Through darkest storms, we find the way,
In faith's embrace, we choose to stay.
The silent prayers, like stars ignite,
In shadows cast, we claim the light.

For every burden, lifted high,
In mercy's arms, our spirits fly.
Within the night, a promise glows,
In shadows blessed, true love bestows.

Hymns of the Brokenhearted

In shadowed valleys, hearts do weep,
A prayer for solace, a promise to keep.
The light may dim, but hope remains,
In silent echoes, love sustains.

With trembling hands, we seek the dawn,
In whispered hymns, our fears are drawn.
A chorus formed from pain's embrace,
Each tear a note in mercy's grace.

Through shattered dreams, we find our way,
In every night, there comes a day.
The brokenhearted rise anew,
In faith's embrace, we start anew.

Oh, guide us in our darkest hours,
With gentle strength, like blooming flowers.
For every wound, a tale to tell,
In love's pure light, we learn to dwell.

So let us sing in voices clear,
A melody of hope, not fear.
From brokenness, we come alive,
In hymns of love, our spirits thrive.

The Divine in Despair

In moments heavy with despair,
We lift our eyes to seek what's fair.
A whisper soft, the soul's embrace,
In silent tears, we find His grace.

The trials faced, our hearts laid bare,
And yet within, a breath of air.
Through darkest nights, a glimmer shines,
His love surrounds, as fate aligns.

In pain we learn, in loss we grow,
The seeds of faith begin to sow.
With every heartache, strength we gain,
From the divine, we rise again.

A fragile journey, but oh so sweet,
In every stumble, His hands we meet.
In despair's grip, we find the light,
Leading us forth from endless night.

Through valleys low to mountains high,
His promises uphold the sky.
For in all fears, we find repair,
The divine presence, always there.

Blessings Wrapped in Grief

In sorrow's arms, we learn to hold,
The blessings wrapped in tales of old.
Each tear that falls, a precious gift,
In mourning's depth, our spirits lift.

For every loss, a heart reborn,
In shadows cast, the light is worn.
Through grief's embrace, we see the truth,
The promise kept in love's sweet youth.

In every heartbeat, echoes sway,
Reminding us that love won't fray.
Through heavy clouds, we seek the sun,
In grief, we find our battles won.

So let us cherish every scar,
The paths we've walked, both near and far.
In blessings found, we honor loss,
For in His love, we bear the cross.

With gentle hands, we mend the soul,
In grief we dance, we become whole.
Embracing all that once was done,
Blessings wrapped in grief, still run.

Faith Amidst the Fracture

In fractured dreams, we search for light,
A spark of faith within the night.
With every crack, new hope ignites,
Guiding our hearts to higher heights.

Amidst the chaos, truth will rise,
In darkest moments, see the skies.
For every fracture tells a tale,
Of love enduring, bold and frail.

With trust we stand, though torn apart,
In every heartbeat, hope will start.
The storms may rage, but we will sing,
In faith's embrace, the peace it brings.

Through trials faced, our spirits soar,
In every wound, we learn to bore.
For faith amidst the fracture bright,
A guiding star in endless night.

So, let us weave a tapestry,
Of grace and strength, a legacy.
In unity found, we carry forth,
Faith amidst the fracture, our worth.

Whispers of the Wounded Heart

In silence speaks the weary soul,
A prayer for solace, to be made whole.
With echoes lingering in the night,
Hearts seek the dawn, a glimmer of light.

The burdened path shows trials faced,
Yet love's warm glow, a steady grace.
In shadows deep, faith's ember glows,
Courage blooms where compassion flows.

Tears like rivers wash the pain,
In holy waters, souls find gain.
Each whisper soft, a guiding hand,
In God's embrace, forever stand.

With every breath, a promise shared,
In sorrow's depth, the heart is bared.
As hymns of hope through darkness rise,
A wounded heart breaks through the skies.

In unity, we rise and call,
To heal the wounded, one and all.
The sacred bond, our love imparts,
In whispers sweet of wounded hearts.

Veils of Sorrow's Embrace

Beneath the veils of sorrow's grace,
We find the light in a hidden place.
With tender hands, we lift the shroud,
To glimpse the hope, so soft and proud.

The weight of grief, a heavy chain,
Yet in each tear, a sacred rain.
In shadows cast by memories dear,
The heart learns strength, despite the fear.

A silent prayer drifts through the air,
Each note a balm, a answered prayer.
As darkness stirs, we hold onto light,
With faith, we walk into the night.

The dance of loss, a tragic song,
Yet through the pain, we grow more strong.
In sorrow's arms, love finds its place,
Each tear we shed, a touch of grace.

Together bound by threads of pain,
In shared lament, we break the chain.
In whispered hope, the veils retreat,
And in our hearts, forever beat.

Echoes in the Temple of Grief

In the temple where shadows dwell,
Echoes of sorrow weave a spell.
Each whispered prayer, a fragile plea,
In the quiet, our souls can see.

The altar stands, aged and worn,
Beneath its weight, hopes are reborn.
With every tear, a story flows,
In silent reverence, love still grows.

Through darkest nights, we seek the light,
Guided by stars, our hearts take flight.
In the temple, our burdens laid,
A sacred bond, in grief displayed.

The echoes call, both soft and strong,
In each refrain, we sing along.
The spirit moves, a gentle breeze,
Comfort found in shared unease.

As candles burn, the shadows fade,
In love's embrace, our fears are stayed.
In the chapel of our deepest sighs,
The temple of grief lifts us to the skies.

Sacrament of Unspoken Pain

In the stillness of the night,
Lies unspoken sorrow, taking flight.
A sacrament, both dark and pure,
Within our hearts, a silent cure.

Each scar a testament of strife,
In shadows deep, we find new life.
With whispered hopes and dreams in tow,
Through pain we learn, through loss we grow.

The chalice raised, we toast the loss,
In unity, we bear the cross.
Each moment shared, a sacred thread,
In silence held, the words unsaid.

Through trials faced, our spirits soar,
In every ache, love's echo pours.
The sacrament, a bond so real,
Together, we learn how to heal.

From whispered prayers to shared grace,
In our embrace, we find our place.
In unspoken pain, we reveal
The strength of hearts that learn to heal.

The Sacred Stream of Loss

In the twilight, whispers call,
Glimmers of hope begin to fall,
A stream flows deep, through dreams once cast,
Reflecting shadows of the past.

Hearts entwined in silent prayer,
Amongst the echoes, find us there,
A testament to love's great cost,
In the sacred stream of loss.

The sorrows linger in the night,
Searching for the distant light,
Each tear a pearl, a lesson learned,
A heart once bright, now softly burned.

Yet in this path of grief we tread,
New blooms shall rise where we have bled,
For loss can give a deeper grace,
In every heart, a sacred space.

Together still, through joy and strife,
We carry forth the gift of life,
In memory's embrace, we find
The sacred stream that binds the mind.

Prayers of a Wanderer

Upon the hills, beneath the skies,
A wanderer lifts their humble cries,
With every step, they seek the light,
In prayers whispered through the night.

The stars above, a guiding grace,
Each twinkle holds a sacred place,
Echoes of dreams yet to unfold,
In the warmth of stories told.

With every breath, a promise made,
The wanderer's faith shall never fade,
In the wind, their solace found,
In sacred whispers, love astounds.

Mountains towering, rivers wide,
In nature's arms, where truth abides,
Their spirit soars, the heart so free,
Lost in the vast infinity.

A journey long but never lone,
In every prayer, a seed is sown,
For in the path, joy intertwines,
In the wanderer's heart, hope shines.

Echoes of Love and Longing

In twilight's glow, two shadows blend,
An echo speaks, a silent friend,
Love's sweet laughter fills the air,
In every dream, your spirit's there.

A heart laid bare, with trembling sighs,
Through all the nights, beneath the skies,
Each whispered name, a prayer of grace,
In every tear, your soft embrace.

Across the miles, love knows no bounds,
In silent spaces, still it sounds,
A melody of souls that yearn,
In every lesson, hearts will learn.

The moon a witness to our plight,
As stars align in the velvet night,
In longing's depths, our spirits soar,
For love's sweet echoes, we explore.

Through storm and calm, we're never lost,
Together still, we bear the cost,
Two hearts entwined, though far apart,
In echoes true, we feel the heart.

The Path of Sacred Suffering

In valleys low where shadows creep,
The path of suffering runs deep,
Yet in the trial, grace takes form,
A gentle light amidst the storm.

Through every tear, a lesson grows,
In pain, the spirit learns to glow,
For every cross we bear alone,
In darkest nights, our hearts have grown.

Each burden shared, a sacred gift,
Uniting souls, our spirits lift,
Through fire and ash, we find our way,
From sacred suffering, hope shall sway.

In stillness found, we seek the dawn,
The promise of a love reborn,
Through trials fierce and shadows long,
In suffering, we find our song.

So walk this path where faith ignites,
In every struggle, find the light,
For love will guide us through the fray,
On sacred paths, we learn to pray.

Beneath the Veil of Sorrow

In the quiet night where shadows creep,
A weary heart, in pain, shall weep.
Yet in this dark, a whisper sings,
Of hope that only the faithful brings.

Each tear a prayer, each sigh a plea,
In spirit's grasp, we long to see.
For every burden, love's light shines,
And in our trials, grace aligns.

Beneath the veil, a promise stays,
The dawn shall break, in wondrous rays.
Though sorrow grips, and shadows loom,
Joy will rise, dispelling gloom.

In faith we stand, though storms may rage,
Transcending pain, we turn the page.
For in our grief, His presence near,
The soul finds peace, and love draws near.

Lamentations of the Soul

In silent rooms where echoes nest,
The troubled heart finds no sweet rest.
A gentle prayer, a heavy sigh,
In longing dreams, we search the sky.

A broken spirit, a fractured song,
Yet in this anguish, we still belong.
For in our sorrows, grace will flow,
And light through darkness begins to grow.

With every lament, a truth unfolds,
In trials faced, our faith beholds.
For every tear that stains the night,
Hope is born, a radiant light.

We rise from ashes, we stand, we claim,
In suffering's depths, we call His name.
Each heartache a stone, a path we tread,
Towards the promise, where angels tread.

Grace in the Heartache

When burdens bear upon the soul,
And dreams once bright begin to bowl.
We search for grace amidst the tears,
In darkest nights, He calms our fears.

Each moment weighed with heavy cost,
Yet in this trial, we are not lost.
For every ache, a lesson learned,
In heartache's fire, the spirit's burned.

The heart finds strength it did not know,
In gentle whispers, love's soft glow.
Though shadows linger, hope draws near,
In grace, we rise, dispelling fear.

For heartache, too, can bear the prize,
Transforming pain to clearer skies.
In every struggle, we find our way,
To brighter dawns and bolder days.

Light Beyond the Shadows

In the depths of night, where darkness reigns,
A flicker calls through all the pains.
For every shadow, a light will break,
Through faith's embrace, our hearts awake.

We seek the path where love will lead,
In every sorrow, a planted seed.
With every step, we rise anew,
In dawn's first light, the world breaks through.

From shadows deep, our spirits soar,
With every heartbeat, we long for more.
Hope rekindled, with strength we fight,
For beyond the pain lies purest light.

So let us walk where visions glow,
Embracing love as we let go.
For in the light beyond the dark,
The soul shall sing, igniting spark.

They Who Mourn find Faith

In shadows deep where sorrows dwell,
A whisper calls from heaven's well.
Through tears that fall, a path unfolds,
In mourning hearts, His love enfolds.

Each heavy sigh, a prayer of trust,
In brokenness, find faith robust.
For in the depths, hope's light will gleam,
Through darkest nights, we hold the dream.

Though trials steep may weigh us down,
With every tear, the grace is found.
In solace sought, a flame ignites,
A boundless love through endless nights.

So lift your gaze from pain's embrace,
And seek the warmth of His sweet grace.
For those who mourn will surely see,
The blessed joy of faith's decree.

In every loss, a promise grows,
In shattered dreams, His mercy flows.
With faith as guide, we'll rise anew,
For He who mourns is cherished too.

In the Garden of Silent Longing

In the garden where shadows weep,
A heart in yearning, secrets keep.
Among the blooms, a sacred song,
In silent longing, we belong.

Soft petals fall like whispered prayers,
Caressed by hope, the soul repairs.
Each rustling leaf echoes the plea,
In solitude, we seek to see.

Beneath the trees, where spirits dwell,
A love that heals, a tale to tell.
In fragrant dusk, the light will guide,
Through each shadow, He walks beside.

So wander deep through sacred ground,
In every silence, peace is found.
For in the stillness, hearts will rise,
Within the garden, faith replies.

When sorrow lingers, joy will bloom,
In longing's arms, dispel the gloom.
A tapestry of heart and mind,
In the garden, our truth we'll find.

Light Streamed Through the Cradle of Suffering

In the cradle where darkness lay,
Light streamed forth, dispelling gray.
Through trials faced and burdens borne,
Hope's gentle glow, a promise sworn.

Each teardrop's fall, a healing rain,
In suffering's grip, love breaks the chain.
With hands outstretched to guide the lost,
In pain's embrace, we'll count the cost.

The morning breaks with tender grace,
As shadows flee from love's warm face.
Through every wound, redemption streams,
In light divine, we find our dreams.

In every heart, a flicker resides,
That through the storm, in faith abides.
As light descends on weary souls,
In suffering's cradle, joy consoles.

So hold the light, let courage soar,
For in the dark, He opens doors.
From every sorrow, rise and sing,
In the cradle, hope's offering.

Within the Ruins, Faith Blossoms

In ruins left by time's cruel hand,
Amidst the dust, we choose to stand.
For in the wreckage, seeds will sprout,
In broken places, love's shout.

The stones may crumble, spirits ache,
Yet faith endures, the world we make.
Through every loss, resilience grows,
In each despair, the beauty flows.

Though shadows loom where hope has fled,
In darkest nights, our hearts are led.
With every breath, we lift our voice,
In ruins deep, we still rejoice.

The path may wind through trials steep,
Yet in our hearts, His promise keeps.
For faith is born in weary eyes,
From every fall, we learn to rise.

So tend the soil of love and grace,
In every ruin, find His face.
For within the wreckage, we discover,
In faith's embrace, we are each other.

The Crossroads of Tears and Triumph

At the dawn of sorrow's grip,
Faith whispers soft, yet bold.
A heart that aches in shadows deep,
Sees light in stories told.

In valleys where the lost have wept,
Hope springs like flowers rare.
Unity in pain is kept,
As spirits rise in prayer.

The weight of burdens, heavy, frail,
Is lifted through the pain.
With every tear, a holy trail,
To joy born of disdain.

A journey carved in strife and grace,
Where tears and triumph blend.
In every heart, a sacred space,
Where beginning meets the end.

Beyond the crossroads, deep within,
The soul begins to soar.
For every loss, a chance to win,
In love's forevermore.

Anchored in Divine Mourning

In shadows cast by grief's embrace,
We seek the strength to cope.
With every tear upon our face,
We anchor deep in hope.

A heart that mourns is not alone,
For angels softly sing.
In every sigh, a love that's known,
As chains of sorrow cling.

We gather in the quiet night,
As stars above us weep.
In darkness, we find sacred light,
And solace for the deep.

For in the depths of our despair,
The divine reaches near.
In mourning's grasp, we find the care,
That binds our broken years.

Each moment spent in soulful prayer,
Is balm for wounded souls.
In shared grief, the burdens share,
As love and faith make whole.

Soft Echoes of Merciful Love

In gentle whispers, grace draws near,
A song of solace strong.
With every note, we cast our fear,
Embraced where we belong.

The heart that knows a love so pure,
Resounds in every sigh.
In moments brief, we find the cure,
As mercies never die.

Through trials faced and wounds that bleed,
Compassion's voice survives.
In kindness sown, a loving seed,
In every heart, it thrives.

With every echo, soft and warm,
We turn our eyes to grace.
In every storm, love's sacred calm,
Invites us to embrace.

So linger in the tender light,
Where every soul can heal.
In echoes soft, we find the right,
And learn to love, to feel.

The Broken Pottery of Existence

In fragments lay our stories told,
Each shard a life once bright.
In broken pottery, we behold,
The beauty of our fight.

Shattered vessels but not in vain,
Each crack a lesson learned.
For what has shattered can remain,
A light that's brightly burned.

From ashes rise the hopes we cling,
As every piece finds worth.
In every heart, a song can sing,
Of love throughout the earth.

We gather shards, with care and grace,
To craft anew our fate.
In brokenness, we find our place,
And weave our hearts straight.

For in each flaw, a story gleams,
Reflecting who we are.
Through broken pottery, dreams redeem,
And shine like every star.

Illuminated by Struggles

In trials deep, our faith ignites,
A beacon shines through darkest nights.
Each struggle faced, a lesson learned,
In fires of life, our spirits burned.

With every tear, a strength is born,
A path transformed, from rose to thorn.
The weight we bear, our souls refine,
In shadows cast, His love will shine.

Beneath the weight of burdensome days,
We find the light in gentle rays.
For in the depths, where pain does dwell,
His whispers guide, we rise, we swell.

Together walk, through stormy skies,
With heavy hearts, we shall arise.
For every trial, a prayer is sown,
In struggles faced, our faith is grown.

So carry on, through night and day,
For hope will light the weary way.
In every fight, our spirits soar,
Illuminated, forevermore.

Carried by Angels' Hands

In moments fraught with doubt and fear,
They lift us high, their voices clear.
Through stormy seas and tempest's roar,
With angels' hands, we find our shore.

A gentle touch in times of pain,
Reminds us of the love we gain.
In silent prayers, their wings enfold,
Carried softly, our spirits uphold.

With every step, they guide our way,
In shadows deep, they bid us stay.
Through trials faced, we've not alone,
As angels' song becomes our own.

In whispers sweet, they share our cry,
A heart of grace, they never shy.
As burdens lift, our spirits rise,
With wings of faith, we touch the skies.

So let us trust in love's embrace,
In every struggle, find our place.
Carried forth by hands divine,
We walk in light, forever shine.

The Journey of the Forgotten

In shadows cast, where silence lies,
The weary souls, their spirit sighs.
With heavy hearts, they tread the way,
The journey marked in shades of gray.

With voices small, they seek to speak,
In broken dreams, the lost and weak.
Among the throng, they fade from view,
Yet still they hope for something true.

In forgotten paths, the weary tread,
Their hearts a map of tears once shed.
For every step, a prayer in place,
The journey holds the heart's embrace.

In family ties long severed tight,
In distant echoes, they seek the light.
For every heart left in the dark,
Shall rise anew, a hidden spark.

So let us seek the ones unheard,
Extend our hands, share every word.
In love's embrace, we find the way,
The journey long, yet bright each day.

In the Garden of Grief

In tender soil, our sorrow grows,
Among the thorns, the heartache flows.
With every tear, a bloom may rise,
In grief's embrace, the spirit cries.

Each petal soft, a memory dear,
A whispered prayer amidst the fear.
In shadows deep, the flowers sigh,
As seasons change, we learn to fly.

Through weeping willows, we find peace,
In every loss, the wounds may cease.
For in the grasp of darkened nights,
The stars will shine, our hope ignites.

In the garden where we grieve,
Each tender shoot, we shall believe.
In every storm that shakes the heart,
A new beginning, a brand new start.

So let us walk this sacred ground,
Among the blooms, our love is found.
In gardens lush, where pain has ceased,
We find the strength, and know the peace.

The Breath of God in Grief's Grasp

In shadows deep, where sorrows dwell,
The Breath of God, a whispered spell.
Each tear that falls, a sacred place,
Transforms our grief to boundless grace.

With heavy hearts, we seek the light,
In darkened times, His love ignites.
From ashes raised, in faith we stand,
The Breath of God, a guiding hand.

Through valleys low and mountains high,
His presence soothes, we will not cry.
As morning dawns with tender hue,
The Breath of God makes all things new.

When burdens weigh and spirits tire,
His breath ignites a holy fire.
In every loss, a promise sown,
The Breath of God will lead us home.

So let your sorrow find its peace,
In gentle whispers, grief will cease.
For even in the darkest night,
The Breath of God brings forth the light.

Celestial Waters of Liquid Light

From heavens high, the waters flow,
Celestial Light, our hearts bestow.
In every wave, a promise shines,
Refreshing souls and sacred lines.

These liquid jewels, a soft caress,
In trials faced, they bring us rest.
With every drop, a blessing pours,
Celestial waters cleanse our shores.

As rain descends on thirsty ground,
In silence heard, His grace is found.
We lift our eyes to skies so bright,
Celestial waters, pure delight.

In joyful streams, our sorrows drown,
The Light that lifts, no heart can frown.
With faith immersed, we rise above,
Celestial waters, endless love.

So drink deeply, O weary soul,
In flowing streams, we are made whole.
For every wave reflects His might,
Celestial waters of purest light.

The Divine Hand in Sorrow's Grasp

When sorrow grips, and shadows close,
The Divine Hand, our only pose.
In aching hearts, His touch we feel,
A balm to wounds that time will heal.

Through stormy seas and darkest night,
The Divine Hand brings forth the light.
With gentle strength, He holds us near,
In sorrow's grasp, we need not fear.

Each trial faced, a bridge we cross,
The Divine Hand, through pain and loss.
In quiet moments, strength unfolds,
Guiding us through with hands of gold.

Though tears may fall like rain above,
The Divine Hand cradles our love.
In every heartache, faith persists,
The Divine Hand, we cannot resist.

So trust the path where shadows play,
The Divine Hand will guide the way.
Through every trial, we shall rise,
In sorrow's grasp, new hope will rise.

Blessings Born from the Boughs of Heartache

In branches low, where sorrow clings,
Blessings born, the heartache sings.
Each tear a fruit, both sweet and sour,
From pain we grow, through every hour.

The boughs that bend in winds of fate,
Bear fruits of hope, though hearts await.
In darkest nights, the stars align,
Blessings born from heartache's vine.

With every gust that shakes our soul,
We gather strength to stay whole.
In whispered prayers, the spirit grows,
Blessings bloom where heartache flows.

Through trials faced, the roots run deep,
In faith we stand, our souls in keep.
For from the storms, new life shall rise,
Blessings born beneath the skies.

So let us cherish every plight,
For heartache's weight brings forth the light.
In every loss, we find our way,
Blessings from heartache, come what may.

Miracles in Mourning

In shadows deep, we seek the light,
A whisper of hope, through the night.
Tears like raindrops fall from grace,
Yet love transcends the darkest place.

Each sorrow holds a sacred sign,
In loss, we may yet find divine.
A garden blooms where ashes lie,
Miracles grow from grief's soft sigh.

Embrace the pain, let it be shared,
For in our hearts, we are ensnared.
Through every trial, the spirit flies,
In mourning's clasp, the soul belies.

Through faith we rise, from shadows bleak,
With every tear, the heart will speak.
A tapestry of joy and strife,
In miracles, we find our life.

Together bound, we walk the road,
With every step, we lighten the load.
In mourning's depth, we'll find a way,
To cherish love, come what may.

Celestial Comfort

Beneath the stars, we find our peace,
In silent prayers, our fears release.
The universe cradles, vast and bright,
A gentle touch in the still of night.

From heavens high, a light descends,
A love so pure, that never ends.
In quiet moments, our souls unite,
Together basking in holy light.

With every breath, we feel the grace,
In trials faced, we find our place.
Upon the wings of faith we soar,
In celestial arms, forevermore.

When burdens weigh and shadows loom,
Look to the skies, dispel the gloom.
For comfort whispers in the air,
Our spirits lifted by love's care.

In unity, we find the thread,
Life's tapestry woven, love widespread.
In every heart, a beacon shine,
Celestial comfort—forever mine.

Reflections on a Tear-stained Journey

Upon the road, we tread so slow,
With tear-stained cheeks, our hearts aglow.
Each drop reflects a path unclear,
Yet hope remains, forever near.

In every sorrow, a lesson learned,
Through trials faced, the spirit burned.
A journey marked by love and pain,
In every heartbeat, life's refrain.

With shadows cast, we brave the night,
Seeking solace in the light.
Each step we take, a prayer we raise,
In faith we walk, through nights and days.

As dawn appears, the tears may dry,
Yet in their wake, we learn to fly.
With strength reborn, we carry on,
Reflections shine when night is gone.

Together we rise, through joy and woe,
In bonds of love, our spirits grow.
A tear-stained journey leads us home,
In faith's embrace, we're never alone.

The Pilgrim's Wail

In weary steps, the pilgrim cries,
With heavy heart and hopeful sighs.
Each winding path and rugged stone,
A testament of battles shown.

Through valleys deep and mountains high,
We wander on, though spirits die.
Yet in the darkness, voices call,
The sacred promise, guiding all.

With every wail, a prayer ascends,
For love to heal what life intends.
The burdens share, through tears receive,
In faith we trust, and we believe.

In search of light, we face the storm,
In every trial, our hearts transform.
The pilgrim's path may twist and turn,
Yet in each trial, the soul will learn.

Through every step, the journey's grace,
In sorrow's arms, we find our place.
Together bound, we wail and sing,
In the pilgrim's heart, new hope shall spring.

Between the Cracks of Despair

In shadows deep where sorrows dwell,
Faith whispers soft, 'All will be well.'
Through trials faced, the heart shall mend,
A light will rise, with love to send.

When doubt creeps in to mask the day,
Hope stands firm, it will not sway.
With every tear that falls like rain,
A promise blooms, through all the pain.

In silence loud, the soul will find,
An inner peace, a strength entwined.
Like roots that grasp beneath the ground,
In every crack, God's grace is found.

Though storms may rage and winds may howl,
In prayer, we hear the comforting vowel.
Every whisper, every plea,
Brings forth the dawn, sets free the sea.

So rise above the weight of night,
For in the dark, there shines the light.
Through trials faced and joys declared,
Between the cracks, our hearts are bared.

The Altar of Abiding Hope

In faith we gather, hand in hand,
Our voices rise, a mighty band.
Upon this altar, dreams lay bare,
With open hearts, we lift a prayer.

Through every struggle, every strife,
Hope leads us onward, giving life.
In gentle whispers, angels call,
Each step we take, we shall not fall.

The weight of burdens, heavy, still,
Transform our hearts, bend to His will.
With open arms, love we embrace,
At this altar, we find our place.

In unity, our spirits soar,
Through every challenge, we'll restore.
Our faith ignites like stars at night,
In darkness found, He is our light.

So here we stand, with courage bright,
Embracing hope, we share the light.
Together bound, we will not break,
An altar built for love's own sake.

Beneath Celestial Anguish

Underneath the heavens vast,
We seek solace, our shadows cast.
With every struggle that we bear,
The stars above become our prayer.

In moments lost, we search for grace,
Within the silence, we find His face.
Each tear a glimmer in the night,
A testament to faith's true light.

Beneath the pain, a beauty grows,
In every heartache, love bestows.
Though often chained to earthly woe,
The spirit learns, and faith will flow.

Celestial anguish, a burden light,
Each trial faced brings forth the bright.
In unity, we rise from plight,
Our souls set free, aflame with might.

So let us stand and face the skies,
With open hearts and sparkling eyes.
For in the depths, the heavens sing,
A hope renewed, on faith we cling.

Lamentations in the House of Prayer

In quiet corners, voices rise,
Lamentations fill the skies.
Each echo speaks of burdens held,
In this house, our sorrows meld.

With every candle lit so high,
We mourn the dreams that passed us by.
Yet in our grief, a seed is sown,
A promise blooms, we're not alone.

We gather here, hearts intertwined,
In shared sorrow, our souls aligned.
Each prayer a thread, each tear a plea,
In the warmth of love, we find our key.

The walls may weep from tales they hold,
Yet faith stands firm against the cold.
In unity through trials shared,
In this house, we're truly bared.

So let us lift our voices loud,
In lamentations, we are proud.
For through our tears, we find the grace,
In the house of prayer, a sacred space.

The Silent Sanctuary of Grief

In shadows deep where sorrows dwell,
The heart finds peace, a sacred shell.
Whispers of love in silence breathe,
In this still space, we gently grieve.

The tears that fall are seeds of hope,
In pain's embrace, we learn to cope.
Faith wraps us in a soft embrace,
In the sanctuary, we find grace.

Time weaves sorrow with tender care,
Each moment shared, a silent prayer.
Through loss, we journey, side by side,
In love's reflection, we abide.

Beneath the weight, our spirits rise,
Through heavy heart, we touch the skies.
In every shadow, light reveals,
The silent sanctuary heals.

In grief's stillness, we become whole,
A tapestry of the human soul.
From brokenness, a strength we glean,
In the silent sanctuary, serene.

Beneath the Wings of Mercy

In the hush of dawn, we find our way,
Beneath the wings of mercy's sway.
The gentle breeze of love's caress,
A refuge found in sweet distress.

With every prayer, our spirits soar,
In mercy's arms, we seek for more.
Forgiveness blooms like flowers rare,
In humble hearts, we cast our care.

The light of grace breaks through the night,
Guiding lost souls toward the light.
In unity, we raise our song,
Beneath the wings, we all belong.

Each act of kindness, a sacred thread,
Woven in love where angels tread.
Trusting in mercy, we find our peace,
From burdens heavy, we find release.

In every heart, a spark ignites,
Beneath mercy's wings, hope excites.
Together we stand, no longer weary,
In love's embrace, our souls grow cheery.

Revelations in Ruin

In the ashes of despair, we seek,
Revelations whispered soft, yet meek.
From broken stones of days gone by,
New truths emerge, as spirits fly.

Through shattered dreams, the light breaks free,
Ruin becomes our destiny.
In silence speaks the haunted past,
Echoes of faith that ever last.

From barren ground, the flowers bloom,
In every heart, a seed of room.
What once was lost, now takes its shape,
In ruin's grace, we find escape.

The trials faced in darkest night,
Reveal the path toward the light.
With every trial, our spirits grow,
Through revelations, love will flow.

In the ruins, beauty does arise,
A testament beneath the skies.
From brokenness, we rise as one,
In the dawn of hope, we are reborn.

Tribulations and Triumphs

In tribulations, our faith is tried,
Yet through the storm, we won't divide.
With heavy hearts, we lift our song,
In trials faced, we grow both strong.

Each struggle shapes the souls we are,
Guiding us gently, like a star.
Through the valleys, we find our way,
Emerging brighter, come what may.

In every moment, a lesson learned,
As fierce as fire, our hearts have burned.
From ashes rise, we claim our right,
In unity, we find our light.

The journey marked by pain and strife,
Leads us to a more fruitful life.
With open hearts and hands held high,
In faith, we reach toward the sky.

For in the end, what we withstand,
Becomes the strength on which we stand.
In every trial that we endure,
We find our triumph, rich and pure.

Heavenly Hues of Heartache

In shadows deep, my spirit weeps,
Yet in pain, a promise keeps.
Each tear a sigh, a silent prayer,
In sorrow's grip, I find Him there.

The heavens weep, they know my plight,
A tapestry of day and night.
With every loss, I learn to see,
The love that flows, it sets me free.

Though heartache sings a mournful tune,
I find my peace beneath the moon.
In every crack, His light breaks through,
A canvas painted with heavenly hues.

The sacred wounds, they bear His name,
Through suffering, I rise, aflame.
In every shadow, grace does flow,
A testament to love I know.

So when the night feels dark and cold,
Remember, faith can be so bold.
With every heartache, a seed is sown,
In the garden of grace, we are never alone.

Illuminated by Pain

In valleys low, the heart does ache,
Yet through the cracks, light starts to break.
Every wound, a story penned,
To show the way, our souls to mend.

Beneath the weight, I stumble, fall,
But in the struggle, I hear the call.
A whisper sweet, in darkest night,
Illuminated by pain, I find the light.

With every sigh, a lesson learned,
In embers low, my spirit burned.
Strength forged in fire, a holy dance,
I rise anew, reborn by chance.

The cross I bear, a sacred gift,
Through every burden, my soul will lift.
In pain's embrace, I feel His grace,
Illuminated love, I long to trace.

So sing, O heart, through trials faced,
In every moment, be interlaced.
For pain is but a passageway,
To joy that dawns with each new day.

Seraphic Solace

In whispers soft, the angels sing,
Of solace found in sacred spring.
Through trials vast and shadows cast,
Their light shines bright, holding fast.

In weary hearts, distress may dwell,
But heavenly peace weaves a spell.
Each breath we take, a prayer so pure,
In seraphic arms, we feel secure.

When storms arise and faith does wane,
A gentle hand soothes every pain.
In times of doubt, they guide the way,
With tender love, our fears allay.

Embrace the night, for morning comes,
The music sweet of quiet drums.
A symphony of hope and grace,
In seraphic solace, we find our place.

So let your heart beat wild and free,
In union sweet, let spirits be.
Together we walk, through dark and light,
In sacred trust, our souls take flight.

The Beauty of the Burden

Each heavy load, a lesson learned,
Through trials faced, my spirit burned.
In struggles fierce, I gain my view,
The beauty of the burden rings true.

When life feels tough and hope seems dim,
I lift my eyes, my heart to Him.
In every weight, I find the art,
Of grace and love that won't depart.

The cross I bear is not so vain,
For every loss gifts strength in pain.
Through sacrifice, I learn to see,
The beauty of the burden in me.

A soul refined like silver bright,
Emerging strong from darkest night.
In every tear, His promise shines,
The beauty of the burden aligns.

So carry on, though heavy the load,
In faith and love, we walk the road.
Each step a testament of grace,
The beauty of the burden we embrace.

Rhapsody of Resilience

In valleys low, where shadows creep,
The spirit stirs, refusing sleep.
With faith as light, the heart will rise,
Embracing hope beneath the skies.

Each trial faced, a lesson learned,
Through storms we walk, our fire burned.
With every tear, a seed we sow,
In gardens bright, our triumphs grow.

The strength within, a sacred song,
In unity, we all belong.
Emboldened souls, with hands entwined,
In love and grace, our hearts aligned.

Through whispered prayers, a guiding star,
We travel paths both near and far.
With faith our shield, we stand as one,
Till shadows fade and light has won.

So let us dance, though trials come,
In rhapsody, our voices hum.
With every step, in grace we tread,
For resilience is a song well-spread.

When Grief Becomes a Gospel

In quiet hours, where sorrow dwells,
A tale unfolds, a heart compels.
From brokenness, new strength to find,
In shadows deep, a light unlined.

We gather stones of love and pain,
A sacred bond from loss we gain.
Each teardrop sings a story true,
In mournful hymns, the soul renews.

When grief unravels, we draw near,
In shared lament, we cast our fear.
With every note, a healing balm,
In the chaos, find a calm.

Let every ache a lesson bring,
In heavy hearts, a cradled spring.
From ashes rise, a chorus loud,
In tender grace, we feel so proud.

Through trials faced, we learn to hold,
The warmth of love, more precious than gold.
In grief's embrace, our spirits soar,
In this gospel, we find much more.

Divine Echoes in the Darkness

When night descends and silence reigns,
In stillness, hear the soft refrains.
The Divine whispers, close and clear,
In darkest void, do not fear.

With each heartbeat, a sacred tune,
Awakens hope beneath the moon.
The echoes of love resonate,
In trials faced, we elevate.

Through shadows cast by doubt and dread,
A path emerges, softly tread.
With faith as compass, eyes aglow,
The heart, a river, learns to flow.

In moments brief, where silence speaks,
In whispered prayers, our spirit seeks.
As stars align, our souls take flight,
In darkness found, we share the light.

And when the dawn begins to break,
In every challenge, hearts awake.
With open arms, we greet the day,
In Divine echoes, find our way.

Broken Halos

In shadows cast by past mistakes,
We wear our wounds, the heart it aches.
Yet from the cracks, a light shall gleam,
In broken halos, hope will beam.

With tender hands, we mend the seams,
Restoring faith in shattered dreams.
For every fall, a chance to rise,
In scars we find our true disguise.

The beauty lies in how we heal,
With open hearts, our truths reveal.
In whispered grace, forgiveness grows,
In brokenness, the spirit flows.

Each halo bent, a tale to tell,
In fractured light, we learn to dwell.
With every tear, a prayer releases,
In gentle souls, our love increases.

So let us stand with hearts expanded,
In broken halos, light commanded.
For in our flaws, we find the whole,
In unity, we heal the soul.

The Hidden Glory in Grief

In shadows deep where sorrows weep,
A spirit sighs, yet hope shall keep.
With every tear, a prayer ascends,
For in the pain, a heart transcends.

The silent cries, a whispered plea,
In loss, we find the mystery.
A sacred space, where love transforms,
In grief, the soul's true beauty warms.

Each heartbeat counts the cost of love,
Awakening the heart above.
In sorrow's depths, a light shall gleam,
For every end begins a dream.

So let the pain be not in vain,
For every loss brings wisdom's gain.
Amidst the dark, we rise anew,
In grief's embrace, our faith breaks through.

The hidden glory shines so bright,
In mourning's depth, there springs the light.
With every trial, we understand,
The beauty found in God's own hand.

From Ashes to Alleluia

From ashes fall, a heart reborn,
In darkest nights, the dawn is sworn.
With every flame that flickers near,
There blossoms hope, dispelling fear.

From dust we came, to dust we go,
Yet in our hearts, the love shall flow.
With every breath that whispers grace,
In trials faced, we find our place.

Through bitter paths, the spirit climbs,
In shattered dreams, new life still shines.
From ashen ground, a flower grows,
With each new song, the spirit knows.

Alleluia breaks the silence deep,
A melody where sorrows sleep.
With every note, we rise and sing,
From ashes, life is blossoming.

Let praises rise, and spirits soar,
In every heart, we seek for more.
From pain to joy, the journey flows,
In every heart, the love still glows.

Dances in the Dark

In shadows cast, the spirit sways,
A dance of hope through night's dark maze.
With every step, the heart does sing,
In silence deep, the angels cling.

Though darkness looms and fears abound,
In hidden places, grace is found.
The rhythm of the soul so pure,
In every struggle, we endure.

Through midnight's veil, the spirit twirls,
In grace unseen, the heart unfurls.
With whispered dreams and faith in flight,
In every tear, we find the light.

So let us dance, though shadows fall,
In every echo, He hears our call.
The unseen joy in trials stark,
A holy hymn, the dances spark.

In every turn, a promise bright,
For in the dark, we find the light.
With every breath, the dawn shall break,
In dances held, our lives awake.

The Pain of Redemption

In trials faced, the heart must break,
For through the pain, the soul awake.
Redemption's path is lined with grace,
In suffering, we find our place.

With every wound, a lesson learned,
From ashes cold, a heart returned.
Through agony, the spirit sighs,
In pain, the truth before our eyes.

The cross we bear, a heavy weight,
Yet leads us to the open gate.
With every scar, a story flows,
Of love enduring, that only grows.

For in the dark, unfold the light,
In every tear, there blooms the right.
Through pain and loss, our spirits rise,
And find redemption in the skies.

So let us wear our scars with pride,
In every struggle, He's our guide.
For through the pain, we come to see,
The beauty born from agony.

Finding Faith in Fragments

In pieces small, my heart does seek,
Each fragment holds a truth unique.
With whispered prayers, I mend the seams,
Finding faith within my dreams.

The cracks reveal a hidden light,
Illuminating darkest night.
In silence, doubt begins to fade,
A tapestry of hope is made.

I gather shards, they spark a flame,
Each broken part becomes a name.
In every loss, a lesson speaks,
The strength to rise when courage seeks.

With gentle hands, I weave my way,
Through shadows where the lost might stray.
Resilience blooms in barren ground,
In faith, our unity is found.

So let these fragments guide my soul,
As I embrace the fleeting whole.
In every piece, a story glows,
Finding faith where spirit flows.

The Altar of the Weeping

Upon this stone, my tears shall fall,
An altar built to heed the call.
In sorrow's grip, I find my prayer,
A silent plea suspended in air.

Each droplet carries weightless fears,
A sacred bond forged through the years.
In vulnerability, I stand,
Before the One who understands.

The quiet echoes of the night,
Bring comfort to my aching plight.
Here in the stillness, I confess,
The burdened heart seeks nothing less.

In grief, a melody begins,
A song of hope where love wins.
I honor pain, yet long for grace,
The altar holds a warm embrace.

Through weeping, healing starts to bloom,
Transforming sorrow into room.
With every tear, a promise made,
The spirit flourishes unafraid.

Threads of Spirit Interwoven

From every weave, a story spun,
In threads of spirit, we are one.
The fabric of our lives entwined,
In sacred patterns, truth defined.

Through trials faced, the fibers strain,
Yet beauty blooms amidst the pain.
In unity, our souls connect,
A tapestry we all reflect.

With gentle hands, we share the load,
Finding strength in this shared road.
Each thread a voice, each stitch a vow,
In love, we knit the solemn now.

With colors bright and shadows deep,
Our journey's tapestry we keep.
In every twist, a lesson learned,
A cherished flame within us burned.

As one we stand, together bold,
Our hearts entwined, a vision told.
In threads of spirit, we ignite,
A dance of faith, a guiding light.

Embracing the Unseen

In silence dwells the mystic grace,
The unseen hand that guides our place.
With open hearts, we learn to see,
The pathways forged by jubilee.

In whispers soft, the spirit moves,
With every breath, our faith improves.
Reality sits beyond the gaze,
Transforming shadows into praise.

The air is thick with hopes untold,
In every moment, truths unfold.
We grasp the light through veils of doubt,
Embracing what our hearts about.

In quietude, the soul takes flight,
Finding strength in the sacred night.
To trust the unseen is our call,
In faith, we rise, we will not fall.

So let us walk where spirits dream,
In realms where love and courage beam.
With open minds, we seek the light,
Embracing all that feels just right.

Milton Keynes UK
Ingram Content Group UK Ltd.
UKHW020039271124
451585UK00012B/950

9 789916 896860